My Family **My Brothers and Sisters**

Emily Sebastian

PowerKiDS press.

New York

Published in 2011 by The Rosen Publishing Group, Inc.
29 East 21st Street, New York, NY 10010

First Edition

Editor: Amelie von Zumbusch
Book Design: Ashley Burrell
Photo Researcher: Jessica Gerweck

Photo Credits: Cover, pp. 5, 7 (dad, mom), 8, 10–11, 13, 16, 20 Shutterstock.com; p. 7 (brother) © www.iStockphoto.com/Ekaterina Monakhova; p. 7 (sister) © www.iStockphoto.com/ quavondo; pp. 14–15 © www.iStockphoto.com/Marilyn Nieves; p. 19 © www.iStockphoto. com/Chang; pp. 22–23 Marilyn Conway/Getty Images.

Library of Congress Cataloging-in-Publication Data

Sebastian, Emily.
  My brothers and sisters / Emily Sebastian. — 1st ed.
      p. cm. — (My family)
  Includes index.
  ISBN 978-1-4488-1463-3 (library binding) — ISBN 978-1-4488-1492-3 (pbk.) — ISBN 978-1-4488-1493-0 (6-pack)
  1. Brothers and sisters. 2. Brothers and sisters—Family relationships. I. Title.
  HQ759.96.S43 2011
  306.875—dc22   9382
                                                    2010007496

Manufactured in the United States of America

CPSIA Compliance Information: Batch #WS10PK: For Further Information contact Rosen Publishing, New York, New York at 1-800-237-9932

Contents

Do you know anyone who has a brother or sister?

This is a **family tree**. As you can see, brothers and sisters have the same **parents**.

Family Tree

Dad

Mom

Brother

Sister

Not everyone has a brother or sister. Isabella is an only child.

Mia and Alicia are **stepsisters**. Many kids have stepbrothers or stepsisters.

Justin and Diego are twin brothers. They were born on the same day.

Families do fun things together. Eva and Eddie go camping.

Ben hurt his knee. His sister Maya took good care of him.

Even though they love each other, brothers and sisters sometimes fight.

Many brothers and sisters take part in family **traditions**, such as dancing.

Brothers and sisters are very important in each other's lives.

Words to Know

family tree (FAM-lee TREE) A chart that shows the members of a family.

parents (PER-ents) Mothers and fathers.

stepsisters (STEP-sis-terz) Girls who became sisters when their parents married each other.

traditions (truh-DIH-shunz) Ways of doing things that have been passed down over time.

Index

Web Sites

Due to the changing nature of Internet links, PowerKids Press has developed an online list of Web sites related to the subject of this book. This site is updated regularly. Please use this link to access the list: www.powerkidslinks.com/family/siblings/